A PORTAL MASTER'S GUIDE TO SKYLANDS

By Barry Hutchison

INSIGHT KIDS
San Rafael, California

GREETINGS FROM MASTER EON

Welcome, young Portal Master. You have made a wise choice by picking up this tome. The pages that follow contain a wealth of knowledge on a subject very close to my heart: that most wondrous realm known as Skylands.

Home to daring heroes, dastardly villains, creatures both adorable and diabolical, and the finest selection of hats you're ever likely to see, Skylands is truly a place filled with magic and wonder.

The book you are currently holding provides one of the most detailed guides to Skylands that can be found anywhere in your world. Whether you're intrigued by the Core of Light, fascinated by Traptanium, or simply wish to get to know Kaos's Mom a little better (although I'm not sure why you would), you'll find the answers you seek within.

Now, I urge you to read on quickly, Portal Master. The forces of darkness are gathering once again, and Skylands is in greater danger than ever. Knowledge is power, and right now we need all the power we can get.

Study this book carefully, learn its many secrets, and prepare for an adventure with Skylands' greatest heroes, the Skylanders!

WHO IS MASTER EON?

Although Master Eon is now considered to be one of the greatest Portal Masters of all time, this wasn't always the case. He began his career as a humble servant, washing and tidying for the Portal Master, Nattybumpo. No one paid the young Eon much notice until the day he accidentally activated a portal and transported a very surprised Nattybumpo into the heart of the Dirt Seas.

In the years that followed, Eon developed his natural talent for controlling portals and rose to become a true champion of all that is good.

Dedicating himself to protecting Skylands, Master Eon is responsible for personally recruiting many of the Skylanders and training them to the peak of their abilities.

While defending the Core of Light from an attack by the evil Kaos, Master Eon was—unfortunately—blasted into his own portal by a huge explosion. There he remains, forever trapped between the worlds, able to appear only in spirit form to offer advice and guidance to any hero brave enough to follow in his footsteps.

WHAT'S ALL THIS PORTAL MASTER STUFF?

Portal Masters are some of the wisest and most powerful beings to have ever inhabited Skylands. Only a rare few who are born with the ability to manipulate portals undergo the necessary training to become a fully-fledged Portal Master, ready to help protect Skylands from the Darkness and all those under its power.

While there were once many Portal Masters working to fight back the Darkness, they were eventually hunted down and defeated until only Master Eon remained. The future of Skylands looked bleak, but a new generation of Portal Masters from Earth are now helping the Skylanders drive back the forces of evil once more.

And it's a good thing, too, because while Master Eon was the last *good* Portal Master, there are a few bad ones lurking out there, too . . .

SKYLANDS

Located at the center of the universe, Skylands is a realm of floating islands with no known beginning or end. A wondrous and magical place, Skylands was created by the Ancients, and each of its islands is a whole new world just waiting to be discovered.

Over the centuries, many fearless—or perhaps foolish—explorers have ventured on their airships into the great beyond, hoping to reach the edge of Skylands and discover what lies beyond. Few of them have ever returned.

While Skylands can be a dangerous place, it is also filled with beauty and wonder. Scattered across its endless islands are awe-inspiring monuments, breath-taking scenery, and a near-infinite number of creatures from the largest Leviathan to the tiniest Chompy.

Although vast areas of Skylands have been explored and documented, even larger areas remain untouched. Who knows what might still be lurking out there waiting for some brave hero—or Portal Master—to discover?

BRAVING THE ELEMENTS

Although the inhabitants of Skylands may appear to all be very different, they actually have a lot in common, as many of them are associated with one of ten Elements. These Elements are an important part of Skylands, giving powers and abilities to those who align themselves with them.

While we currently know of these ten Elements, it is always possible that there may be others out there somewhere just waiting to be discovered. For now, though here's a rundown of those Elements we know about.

AIR

Thanks to Skylands' almost infinite amount of sky, there's plenty of air to go around, and creatures who align themselves with this Element have a near-limitless supply of power to draw from. Air Element Skylanders often perform devastating wind and weather-based attacks from twirling tornados to lethal lightning strikes.

EARTH

Dependable as a rock and most commonly associated with the color brown, you might think Earth is a pretty dull Element. However, Earth-aligned Skylanders can cause ground-shaking earthquakes, use crystal prisms to project energy blasts, and even rain rocks from the sky. Not so boring now, is it?

WATER

No matter where you go in Skylands, you're never far away from a stream, river, waterfall, or ocean, and Water-aligned creatures are a very common sight. The seas of Skylands are home to all manner of beings, and it is from these mysterious depths that many of the most powerful Skylanders have risen.

TECH

Ever felt like a tiny cog in a big machine? You may have a natural affinity with the Tech Element. For thousands of years, the Tech Element went largely unnoticed until an ancient race known as the Arkeyans was able to harness its power, allowing them to create incredible—and often deadly—machines.

FIRE

One of the oldest known Elements of all, Fire dates back to long before Skylands' recorded history began. Over the centuries, its fiery glow has played a vital role in keeping the Darkness at bay. Skylanders associated with this element can be hot-tempered, and their attacks—from molten lava blasts to flaming arrows—can always be counted on to turn up the heat on the forces of evil.

MAGIC

If Tech is the Element most favored by scientists, Magic is the one best suited to wizards and sorcerers. Arguably the most important Element of all, Magic is the force that first created Skylands and now holds it together. As such, Magic Element Skylanders are some of the most powerful heroes of all.

UNDEAD

You'd be forgiven for thinking that those aligned with the Undead Element are likely to be evil, but you'd be wrong. Sure, they might look a bit creepy, smell a bit funny, and sometimes have bits that fall off, but these dark and shadowy heroes play an important part in keeping Skylands safe.

LIFE

Wherever you look in Skylands, you'll find the place teeming with life. From the tallest trees to the smallest saplings, the tiniest bugs to the most enormous sea monsters, Life is everywhere. Skylanders aligned with Life are not just in tune with the Element; they are in tune with all living things and can often call on their help in the heat of battle.

DARK

Discovered after the same explosion that revealed the Light Element, Dark is perhaps the most sinister and dangerous Element of all. As the name suggests, Skylanders aligned with this element are powered by the Darkness itself. Luckily, the heroes have been able to resist the Darkness's temptations and use their power for good.

LIGHT

Although just as ancient as the other Elements, the Light Element was only recently discovered after an explosion ripped open the foundations of Skylands, revealing both Light and Dark Elements. A most useful element when it comes to pushing back the Darkness, Light is a powerful new weapon that heroes and villains alike have been quick to put to use.

THE CORE OF LIGHT

Constructed by a mysterious but kindly race known as the Ancients, the Core of Light is a machine built for the sole purpose of fighting back against the Darkness. Built from the Elements themselves, the Core of Light protected Skylands from the Darkness for centuries until Kaos blew it to bits with a four-headed dragon. Luckily, the Skylanders were able to fix it before the Darkness could consume Skylands for good. As well as directly helping push back the Darkness, the Core of Light has also been known to grant Skylanders special LightCore abilities, making them even more powerful in battle.

THE SKYLANDERS

Over the years, countless numbers of Skylanders have made a stand against the Darkness. Over the next few pages, we'll look at just a few of them.

SPYRO ✶

Quite possibly the most famous hero in all of Skylands, Spyro is a fearless young dragon with a thirst for adventure. Armed with fire breath, a thunderous battering-ram charge, and a photographic memory that allows him to remember the weakness of every villain he has ever encountered, Spyro is a real force to be reckoned with.

Spyro's willingness to hurl himself into danger means he can often find himself in deep trouble. While his stubborn and headstrong nature means he likes to solve his own problems, he also knows he can rely on his friends, the other Skylanders, to help him in times of need.

STEALTH ELF 🍃

Where Spyro likes to run into battle with flames blazing, Stealth Elf prefers a less direct approach. A skilled Forest Ninja, she can slip onto the battlefield and disable her enemies before they even realize she's there and be back at home with her feet up before they figure out what hit them.

That's not to say, though, that she can't handle a straight fight. Her ninja skills are beyond compare, and very few villains can go head-to-head with her without their heads getting very badly bruised. For someone who likes to be subtle, she always speaks her mind—even if she sometimes shouldn't.

ERUPTOR 🔥

Technically, Eruptor is a Lava Monster, but to the untrained eye, he looks like a big chunk of living rock. Fueled by molten magma, the Fire Element, and an explosive temper, Eruptor is renowned for his anger issues, and the last thing you want to do is get on his nerves.

   While not as quick-witted as Spyro or Stealth Elf, Eruptor's brute strength—along with his ability to barf enormous pools of flaming hot lava over enemies—makes him a valuable addition to the team.

POP FIZZ ✹

There are many odd and eccentric Skylanders but only one who's legitimately crazy. Pop Fizz is an alchemist who is rarely seen without some colorful and completely untested potion clutched in his furry blue fingers. He is often mistaken for a gremlin, but the truth is that no one really knows what he is—not even Pop Fizz himself.

Constantly curious and ridiculously reckless, Pop Fizz is always mixing up some new concoction and testing it on himself. Some of his potions grant him incredible powers, while others make him change color, lose his hair, or give him terrible flatulence. Even if his potions aren't always perfect, Pop Fizz himself is the ideal blend of enthusiasm, bravery, and full-blown insanity that makes him one of Master Eon's most prized Skylanders.

JET-VAC ◉

The Sky Barons of Windham are a noble race, and Jet-Vac may just be the most noble of them all. A fully-fledged flying ace, Jet-Vac earned his wings at a young age and wore them proudly. However, when Windham was attacked, Jet-Vac sacrificed his wings so a mother could fly her children to safety.

Although he feared his flying days were over, Jet-Vac's sacrifice was soon rewarded when Master Eon invited him to join the Skylanders. Now, equipped with a vacuum-based jetpack, Jet-Vac soars over Skylands, protecting all those below from the forces of evil and occasionally carrying out some light carpet–cleaning duties.

FLASHWING

No one really knows where Flashwing came from, but most people agree she's one of the most beautiful creatures who ever lived. No one believes this more than Flashwing herself, and she can usually be found hogging the limelight and trying to make herself the center of attention.

A shining, shimmering dragon whose whole body appears to be fashioned from sparkling gemstones, Flashwing can dazzle enemies with both her stunning looks and fighting ability. While she can sometimes be a little obsessed with looking her best, she can always be relied on to help a fellow Skylander in need.

CHOP CHOP

Take a quick glance at Chop Chop, and you might think he's a little creepy. Look again, though, and you'll soon realize the truth: He's *very* creepy. A hybrid of Undead magic and Arkeyan technology, Chop Chop's cold, grating voice and glowing, yellow-eyed stare are enough to frighten most folks. Add in the fact that he's a living skeleton with a very sharp sword, and even the bravest of souls will be off and running.

A former Arkeyan Elite Guard, Chop Chop got bored just hanging about waiting for something to happen, so he set off to wander Skylands in search of his creators, the Arkeyans, who had vanished a long time before. He roamed for a whole century without finding them anywhere before Master Eon decided to put Chop Chop's spooky skills to use as a member of the Skylanders.

GILL GRUNT 💧

When a young, courageous Gillman is in search of adventure, there's only one thing for him to do: Join the Gillman army. That's exactly what Gill Grunt did, and he spent many happy years traveling Skylands with his platoon. During one tour, he met and fell in love with a beautiful mermaid and swore to return to her one day. Unfortunately, when he did, he discovered she'd been kidnapped by pirates.

Determined no one else should have their heart broken by gangs of nasty villains, Gill Grunt joined the Skylanders with whom he now protects mermaids and non-mermaids alike. Gill Grunt enjoys singing, but there is some disagreement over his talent. He thinks he sounds amazing, but everyone else disagrees.

TRIGGER HAPPY

Trigger Happy is a gun-crazed gremlin who thinks the answer to every problem is to shoot it repeatedly. Evil villains attacking town? Fire away! Lid screwed on the peanut-butter jar too tightly? Blast it to bits! Diplomacy is definitely not his strong point.

Highly excitable, Trigger Happy loves to play games. Even more than games, though, he loves to play *tricks* and can often be found hiding sheep for the unsuspecting Hugo to find. With his floppy tongue and erratic behavior, when people see Trigger Happy for the first time, they often think he's completely crazy. And, to be honest, they're probably right.

ROLLER BRAWL

The youngest of a family of vampires, Roller Brawl quickly realized if she was going to compete with her older, much bigger brothers, she'd have to rely on her speed and agility. So impressive were her skills that she was quickly signed up to the Undead Roller Derby League, where she rose to be one of the toughest jammers around.

Life—or *after*life, at least—was good for Roller Brawl until Kaos set eyes on her and immediately fell head-over-heels in love. Her brothers tried to scare him off, but Kaos was undeterred and had them all kidnapped by a Drow army. Now Roller Brawl is dedicated to bringing Kaos down and hopefully finding her brothers in the process.

FRIENDLY FACES

All Skylanders are heroes, but not all heroes are Skylanders.
While none of these guys have joined the ranks of the
Skylanders, they've helped save the day time and time again.

HUGO

This highly intelligent Mabu may be prone
to worrying about silly things and is even a
little cowardly sometimes, but he remains
Master Eon's most reliable advisor and a
trusted friend to the Skylanders.

Whether introducing new recruits to
the academy, helping rebuild the Core
of Light, or discovering secrets
and clues in the library, Hugo
is constantly proving himself
useful. And, although he is
deeply suspicious of sheep and
flees in terror whenever he sees
one, he remains one of the Skylanders'
greatest allies.

FLYNN

The Mabu Flynn is strong, fearless, and
the best pilot in all of Skylands. At least he
insists so, but the number of crashes and
near misses he has had in his airship makes
it difficult to believe.

Always happy to help the Skylanders
out, Flynn is even more than happy to take
credit for their victories, and those who
don't know him could consider him arrogant.
Those who *do* know him could consider him
arrogant, too, because he often is. Still,
despite his brash over-confidence, his
heart is in the right place, and he can
(usually) be counted on to do the
right thing.

CALI

Capable, quick-thinking, and brave, Cali is everything Flynn pretends to be, which may be why he likes her so much. One of Skylands' most courageous explorers, Cali has faced countless dangers, fought all manner of monsters, and loved every minute of it!

Hoping to pass some of her experience on to the Skylanders, she can often be found issuing challenges to the new recruits, helping them train for the battles ahead. Without Cali's help, many of Skylands' greatest heroes would never have unlocked their full potential.

TESSA

The only non-Mabu on our list, Tessa is a fearless fox-girl who has been known to get a little over-excited at times. While she has no special abilities, she arguably has something even better—an enormous bird named Whiskers that she flies around on.

She is no slouch when it comes to battling the forces of darkness and has fought alongside the Skylanders to help thwart Kaos's evil schemes. Loyal and trustworthy, Tessa's willingness to risk her life to protect the inhabitants of the Cloudbreak Islands saw her earn her place as the Chieftess of Woodburrow.

KAOS

What can be said about Kaos that hasn't been said already? He's kind, generous, and a friend to animals everywhere. Those are things that have never been said before, because none of them are true.

Although Kaos calls himself an "evil genius," only one of those words is technically correct. He's definitely evil, no question about that, but calling him a genius is stretching the truth a little.

Yes, he has been known to come up with some utterly diabolical schemes, and yes, his dark magic is a force to be reckoned with, but his blundering arrogance, fiendish lunacy, and comically oversized head mean it is often difficult to take him seriously.

Born into a royal family where he immediately became the ugliest member by a large margin, Kaos was never really appreciated at home and soon set off to make a name for himself—a name that he now enjoys shouting at the top of his voice whenever the opportunity arises.

Kaos has a big head—in every sense. His ego is out of control, and he considers himself the greatest villain in the history of . . . well, everywhere, really. He hates everyone—with the exception of his butler, Glumshanks, who he merely dislikes, and the Skylander Roller Brawl, who he is deeply in love with—and has dedicated himself to bringing pain and misery to Skylands and all who live there.

Despite his evil nature, Kaos has occasionally helped the Skylanders take down other villains in the past, but this was mostly because he didn't think the others were taking their evildoing seriously enough, not because he'd become one of the good guys.

FACT FILE

NAME: Kaos

AGE: Unknown

HEAD SIZE: Enormous

ABILITIES: Powerful sorcerer, evil Portal Master, skilled inventor, giant head projector

WEAKNESSES: Over-confidence, tiny size (except head)

Greetings!

It is I, KAOOOOOOS! I've taken over this idiotic book to tell you about two people who are very important to me—but not in a sissy "feelings" sort of way, bleurgh!—my butler, Glumshanks, and my mom, Mom. Read on

or be destroyed!

GLUMSHANKS

Glumshanks is proud of the fact that he was the first—ever troll to become a butler, even though he only did so because he was useless at doing *real* troll things, like blowing stuff to bits. He still is, actually. You should see him trying to light a stick of dynamite. It's *embarrassing.*

I mean, OK, I'll admit he can be pretty useful to have around sometimes—my socks aren't going to wash themselves, after all—but by and large he's just annoying. He thinks he's sooo clever when he spots the flaws in my *genius* plans and is under the impression

that he's funny just because people laugh at his jokes. They're only laughing out of pity, you blithering fool!

No matter how much I encourage him, Glumshanks never quite manages to be evil enough. In fact, at times he's almost *kind,* but I'm quick to punish him, and I'm still hoping it's just a phase he'll grow out of.

MOM

Now, I'm not saying I'm better and more important than my mother in every possible way, but think about this—most people only ever refer to her as *Kaos's Mom*. Her name, not that anyone really cares, is Kaossandra, but because I'm the famous and important one, it makes sense just to refer to her in relation to me.

An evil Portal Master with powers that (despite what everyone else might say) don't even come close to my own, my mom is annoyingly pleasant to even the most pathetic of her underlings, showing them the kindness and affection she has never once bothered to show me.

Sly(ish) and (a bit) cunning, Mother dreams of taking over Skylands, but she's going to have to get in line, because if anyone is going to summon the Darkness and rule Skylands with a fist of iron, it's me!

IN THE BEGINNING . . .

Just how did the Earth-based Portal Masters get involved with Skylands and its inhabitants? Well, things started something like this:

THE CORE NO MORE

While Master Eon and the Skylanders are sworn to protect all of Skylands, one of their main tasks is to guard the Core of Light. Unfortunately, thanks to Lord Kaos and his four-headed pet dragon, the Hydra, they failed. The Core of Light exploded, taking Master Eon with it. And as for the Skylanders? Well . . .

BANISHED

The force of the magical explosion sent the Skylanders hurtling to planet Earth. With no magic to help give them life, they found themselves frozen in the form of toys. With no one to protect Skylands and no Core of Light to hold back the Darkness, Kaos reigned supreme.

THE RETURN

Fortunately, Master Eon didn't perish in the explosion and instead became a big, shiny, floating head thingy (probably not the technical term). Using some pretty impressive magic, Eon was able to recruit Portal Masters from Earth, and with their help, the Skylanders returned to Skylands!

REBUILDING THE CORE

Without the Core of Light, the Darkness—a malevolent force of pure evil—swept across all of Skylands. The Skylanders' first job was to track down and retrieve the scattered pieces of the core and rebuild it. With the help of Hugo, Flynn, Cali, and a few others, they succeeded, and the rebuilt core quickly drove away the Darkness.

KAAAAAOOOOOOS!

Although the Core of Light was all shiny and new again, the evildoer who had caused all the problems in the first place was still out there. And so, aided by their Earth-bound Portal Masters once more, the Skylanders headed to Kaos's lair to bring him to justice. What they didn't reckon on was the Hydra, and they were thrust into a fight not just for their lives, but for the very future of Skylands.

JUSTICE IS SERVED

Working together, the Skylanders managed to defeat the forces of evil, and Kaos was brought before Master Eon. After Kaos promised to keep attacking Skylands until he ruled it, Eon decided to give him a taste of his own medicine and banished him to Earth. Just like the Skylanders, Kaos found himself turned into a toy and was promptly chewed up by a little dog.

THE END?

It seemed that Skylands was finally safe, but little did anyone suspect, danger was lurking just around the corner . . .

THE ARKEYANS

Once, far back in the mists of time, the Arkeyans were a peaceful race. Vastly intelligent, endlessly curious, and occasionally a little reckless, they quickly began to advance beyond all of the other inhabitants of Skylands. However, it wasn't until they discovered the Tech element and started building wondrous, Magic-fueled machines that things *really* got out of control and their thirst for knowledge became a thirst for power.

Led by their king, the Arkeyans used their advanced intellect and an assortment of diabolical devices to conquer Skylands. Luckily, a band of noble (and enormous) heroes stood against them, and after a series of titanic battles, the reign of the Arkeyan King was brought to an end.

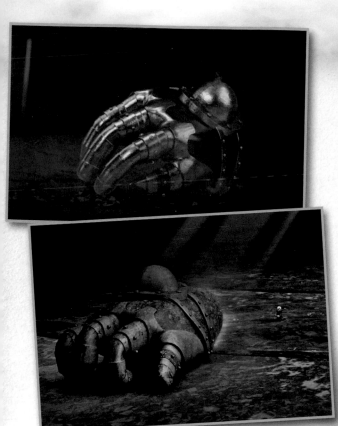

IRON FIST OF ARKUS

A metal gauntlet worn by the Arkeyan King, the Iron First of Arkus was constructed from Tech and Magic and could be used to summon machines, generate force fields, and create Arkeyan warriors. If a non-Arkeyan wore the glove, they would be transformed into a robotic version of themselves, and some experts believe the Iron Fist was a living thing with a mind of its own.

ARKEYAN CONQUERTRON

A massive robot built by the Arkeyans, the Conquertron has a deep respect for anyone interested in causing mayhem and carnage. Despite being incredibly powerful, he is the willing servant of evildoers everywhere and will gladly take part in any villainous schemes he comes across. Over ten thousand years old, the Conquertron was thought lost for most of that time but recently reappeared to cause problems for the Skylanders.

THE GIANTS

Over ten thousand years ago, a band of brave heroes united to fight back against the wicked Arkeyans, who had seized control of Skylands. Known as the Giants—on account of them all being giants—these eight enormous heroes were the first Skylanders and managed to defeat the Arkeyans in a series of epic battles. Afterwards they vanished, never to be seen again. Or at least, that's what everyone thought, but when Kaos roused an ancient Arkeyan Conquertron from its slumber, the Giants returned to protect Skylands once more.

Here are a few of the Giants you might meet while roaming around Skylands. Just be careful you don't get stepped on.

CRUSHER ⛰

As a young giant, Crusher liked to crush, smash, pulverize, and generally destroy things. Of all the things he loved to crush, rocks were his favorite. Armed with his enormous hammer (also named Crusher), he traveled all over Skylands, hammering stones of all shapes and sizes. When he discovered the Arkeyan King was melting rocks for his own wicked ends, though, Crusher discovered there was something he enjoyed smashing even more than rocks—Arkeyan robots!

TREE REX 🍃

As you might expect of someone who is basically a walking, talking tree, Tree Rex is aligned with the Life Element. Once just your average, everyday tree, pollution from an Arkeyan factory seeped into his roots, bringing him to life. Wise, noble, and strong, Tree Rex has dedicated himself to destroying anything that threatens the natural balance of Skylands, while also serving as a pleasant home for birds and other woodland creatures.

NINJINI ✸

Way back before the Arkeyans started getting up to no good, Ninjini was the most powerful magician around. Jealous of Ninjini's magic—and her impressive ninja skills—a dark sorceress trapped her inside an enchanted bottle, where she was meant to stay for all eternity. Ninjini had other ideas, though, and after years of training herself in her bottle to be an even greater warrior, she broke free and dedicated herself to helping those in need—and to ninja-chopping bad guys.

THE SWAP FORCE

The SWAP Force were a group of Skylanders tasked with protecting Cloudbreak Islands and its magical volcano. Once every hundred years, the volcano would erupt, replenishing Skylands' magic.

Following an epic battle with an army of Fire Vipers, the SWAP Force Skylanders were caught in the heart of the eruption. Rather than destroying them, the explosion sent them hurtling to Earth.

The magical eruption changed them, too, granting them new powers and giving them the ability to swap halves with their teammates. This allowed the SWAP Force to create powerful new combinations. These mix-and-match heroes would go on to play a vital role in saving Skylands from the evil Kaos—and his mom.

The force of the explosion scattered chunks of Traptanium all over Skylands and even uncovered two new Elements, Light and Dark. As if that wasn't enough, the explosion also sent the Trap Masters hurtling toward Earth, where they found themselves turned into toys, just like the other Skylanders before them.

TRAPTANIUM

The rare, magic-infused Traptanium is the toughest material to have ever been discovered in Skylands. It was believed to be unbreakable until Kaos proved that theory wrong when he blew Cloudcracker Prison's Traptanium walls to bits.

The shards of Traptanium proved themselves very useful, though, as the Trap Team discovered the substance could be used to capture and hold the essence of defeated villains, just like a portable jail cell.

Trap Masters also use weapons made from Traptanium, which allow them not only to defeat villains, but also to destroy Traptanium barriers and obstacles.

TRAP MASTERS

After the explosion at Cloudcracker Prison sent them to Earth, Master Eon's newly recruited Portal Masters returned the Trap Masters to Skylands, where they set, where they set about helping the Skylanders round up the escaped villains. All the Trap Masters are heroes, but the three below are among the most heroic of all.

GEARSHIFT ⚙

King Mercurus of the Tech island Metallana wanted a daughter. So he built one! The robot, Gearshift, had no interest in swanning around the place being a princess, though, and preferred to spend her time tinkering with the kingdom's huge underground machines and learning how they worked. Her knowledge of the underground tunnels proved invaluable when marauders tried to kidnap her father. Gearshift hid him and led an uprising that drove the marauders away. Gearshift's bravery brought her to the attention of Master Eon, who offered her a place on his Trap Team.

SNAP SHOT 💧

Arguably the most famous Trap Master of all time, Snap Shot is a blue-skinned Crocagator best known for his amazing tracking skills, his hatred of evil, and his very pointy arrows. Born in a remote swamp, Snap Shot spent his days tracking and destroying any wicked critters who tried to get up to no good. After completely clearing the swamp of villains, he set off into the wider world, where he studied archery with the Elves and learned tracking skills from a wolf pack. Soon, he became one of Skylands' most legendary monster-hunters and the ideal leader for Master Eon's newly formed Trap Team.

WALLOP

Wallop was once a simple apprentice weapon-maker living near the lava pits of Mount Scorch. Wielding an enormous hammer in each hand, he was able to turn shapeless lumps of molten metal into the finest and deadliest blades in all the land. However, when a deadly Fire Viper emerged from the volcano and attacked Wallop's village, he discovered a new use for his hammers. After saving the village, he realized his hammers couldn't just make weapons—they could *be* weapons. Swapping them for Traptanium versions, Wallop embarked on a criminal-hammering career as a Trap Master.

MEET THE DOOM RAIDERS

Want to know more about Cloudcracker Prison's most famous—and most dangerous—residents? The information below, taken from the prison guard handbook, should help.

GOLDEN QUEEN

A wicked queen made of solid gold, the aptly named Golden Queen is the leader of the Doom Raiders and can turn her enemies to gold with a single touch. Best avoided, really.

CHOMPY MAGE ⬡

An odd little puppet-wielding wizard, Chompy Mage is not only able to control Chompies, but can turn himself into a giant Chompy, too. Basically, he likes Chompies. A lot.

WOLFGANG 💀

Wolfgang is a werewolf who can make even other werewolves run in fear. Wielding a bone harp, he dreamed of being a musician until he discovered that crime paid better.

DR. KRANKCASE ⚙

Dr. Krankcase quite probably put the "mad" into "mad scientist." The inventor of a green goo that brings evil wooden creatures to life, this is one doctor from whom you don't want a check-up.

CHEF PEPPER JACK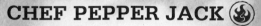

This hot and fiery red pepper enjoys "spicing things up" with exploding vegetables and his deadly egg-beater. Once a renowned chef, the only things he cooks up these days are evil schemes.

DREAMCATCHER

A mischievous floating head who enjoys invading people's dreams and driving them crazy, Dreamcatcher sulks when things don't go her own way, and her tantrums can be lethal.

GULPER 💧

A living blob, Gulper is constantly hungry and will endlessly consume everything in sight, given the chance. When he gulps down soda, he grows in size—and his appetite grows with him.

LUMINOUS

Luminous despises the dark and does everything in his considerable power to drive it away. As well as his light-based attacks, he can shapeshift, allowing him to become anyone he chooses.

NIGHTSHADE 🌙

Already wealthy, Nightshade doesn't steal because he needs to—he does it for fun. Although he appears charming, he is completely heartless and doesn't waste a moment thinking about his victims.

TRAPPABLE VILLAINS

When the Trap Masters were rounding up the Doom Raiders, they encountered several other escaped criminals, too. While not *quite* as deadly as the Raiders, this little lot was still pretty dangerous.

PAIN-YATTA ✳

When Pain-Yatta's best friend, the legendary Unocorn, went missing, the Doom Raiders tricked him into thinking the Skylanders were behind it. He joined the villains and ventured to get revenge on the Skylanders but was eventually captured by the Trap Masters.

BOMB SHELL ✴

For a heavily armored tortoise, Bomb Shell is surprisingly fast on his feet. With a deadly spin-attack that can send foes flying and a worrying number of bombs at his disposal, this is one villain who loves to raise shell.

GRAVE CLOBBER ⛰

He's big, he's bad, and good guys make him mad! Once a great pharaoh, Grave Clobber was recruited by the Golden Queen to help defeat the Skylanders. With his powerful arm-sweep attacks, he proved to be a valuable ally.

BAD JUJU ⊚

If there's one thing the witch-doctor Bad Juju loves, it's an afternoon nap. Anyone who wakes her will incur her terrible wrath and find themselves at the mercy of her weather-based powers.

HOOD SICKLE 💀

A sinister Undead reaper, Hood Sickle is as dangerous as he is creepy. What's more, thanks to his teleportation abilities, he might just be standing behind you right now . . .

BROCCOLI GUY 🌿

While most villains pride themselves on their ability to hurt others, Broccoli Guy's skill lies in healing others. This would be fine, if he didn't insist on healing bad guys and bringing them back from the brink of defeat.

BLASTER-TRON

A high-tech robot from the distant future, Blaster-Tron is armed with advanced laser weaponry and a state-of-the-art rocket pack. He was discovered by the Skylanders when they travelled forward in time to stop Wolfgang.

TAE KWON CROW 🔥 🌙

A skilled ninja and former leader of a band of fearsome Sky Pirates, Tae Kwon Crow—formally known as the "Great Hawkmongous"—is one bird who can get even the bravest heroes in a flap. When not being evil, he enjoys playing Skystones Smash.

THE SUPERCHARGERS

Say what you like about Kaos, but he doesn't give up easily. After being defeated by the Skylanders and Trap Masters, he returned with his most dangerous invention yet: the Doomstation of Ultimate Doomstruction! This giant metal head literally ate the sky, and if you take the sky out of Skylands, well, there's not a whole lot left.

With time running out and the whole of Skylands at stake, a special squad of vehicle-based Skylanders were called on to help save the day. Behold the SuperChargers!

NAME: Spitfire 🔥
VEHICLE: Hot Streak

A fearless speed demon, the flame spirit Spitfire has never *once* lost a race (well, okay, maybe once). As the leader of the Skylanders SuperChargers, Spitfire is always quick to jump behind the wheel of his flame-powered car, Hot Streak, and accelerate towards oncoming danger!

NAME: Stormblade ◎
VEHICLE: Sky Slicer

A fearless explorer with a taste for adventure, Stormblade's wings could never carry her far enough for her liking. Determined to reach the edge of Skylands, she built her ship, the Sky Slicer, only to discover the sky was endless. Now she explores Skylands, looking for people in trouble or bad guys to beat up.

SUPERCHARGING THE SKYLANDERS

When a SuperCharger Skylander hops in their unique signature vehicle, a SuperCharged combination is created, unlocking an exclusive mod that revs up the performance of both the vehicle and the driver!

NAME: Fiesta 💀
VEHICLE: Crypt Crusher

For an Undead guy, Fiesta sure likes to party. The leader of an Undead mariachi band, when Fiesta discovered his former boss was a full-blown bad guy, he helped the Skylanders defeat him. Now he likes to crank up the tunes in his Crypt Crusher car and flatten evil wherever it arises.

NAME: Dive-Clops 💧
VEHICLE: Dive Bomber

Twin brother of the Giant Skylander Eye-Brawl, Dive-Clops might look like a giant eyeball inside a diving suit. That's because that is exactly what he is. Having lost his bat-like wings in a battle with pirates, he now explores beneath the waves in his tank-like submarine, the Dive Bomber, and guards the seas of Skylands.

MINIONS

The creatures that follow have proven themselves to be thorns in the sides of heroes everywhere, but ultimately they're nothing the average Skylander can't easily handle. These are just a few of Skylands' many minions.

CYCLOPSES

Although Cyclopses come in all shapes and sizes, they all have one thing in common. Or, more accurately, one *eye* in common. They also all hate taking baths, which means they all smell pretty bad, so getting close to one is not recommended. Besides, they'd probably try to blow you up.

TROLLS

Although some of the most skilled engineers in Skylands are Trolls, by and large they're not the most intelligent of species. They get their kicks from fighting and blowing things to bits, while they also enjoy drilling for oil, cutting down trees, and other forms of environmental destruction.

GREEBLES

The most miniony of all evil minions, the Greebles are a race of tiny creatures who can be ordered by the dozen from *Minion Monthly* magazine. While not all of them are *bad*, they'll happily do the bidding of even the most wicked of evil villains, and their sheer numbers can cause heroes all sorts of problems.

CHOMPIES

Small, mean, and very, *very* dim-witted, Chompies are little plant-like creatures who use their teeth to give nasty nips to anyone who gets in their way. Individually, they're more annoying than dangerous, but get stuck in a crowd of them, and your ankles will never be the same again.

PIRATES

The plundering and pillaging pirates of Skylands are famed (and feared) all across the eleven seas. As dangerous as they are dirty, these troublesome Sky Bandits spend their days robbing and looting and their nights doing pretty much exactly the same.

DROW

Once proud and noble Elves, the Drow have pledged themselves to the Darkness and become an evil species all of their own. They come in a wide range of types from Spearmen to Witches, and there are also Goliath Drows, who can challenge even the strongest of Skylanders.

MIND MAGIC AND MORE

Even after being defeated *yet again* by the Skylanders, Kaos returned with his most diabolical plan to date—a plan that could tear the very fabric of creation itself in two!

MIND MAGIC

Back when they were first creating Skylands, the Ancients made use of Mind Magic, a mysterious power that granted them the ability to create anything they imagined, which they harnessed within a type of rare, powerful crystal known as Imaginite. After populating Skylands, they realized that if Mind Magic fell into the wrong hands, the results would be catastrophic. They promptly hid it away, only for it to be discovered thousands of years later by a certain big-headed evil genius.

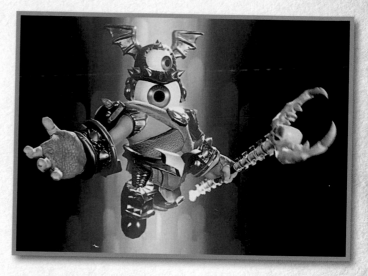

DOOMLANDERS

With the help of Mind Magic, Kaos used his warped imagination to create an army of evil minions he named the Doomlanders. From Brawlers to Sorcerers, Ninjas to Knights, he created a villain for every occasion, and even the mighty Skylanders quickly found themselves overwhelmed.

THE [MOSTLY] SENSIBLE SENSEIS

Each Sensei Skylander has mastered their own unique style of fighting and secret battle technique. For years, their mission was to explore the farthest reaches of Skylands in search of potential heroes to train in the fight against evil. However, once Kaos unleashed Mind Magic and began creating villainous Doomlanders, Master Eon summoned the Senseis to return. They are now leading a new generation of heroes into battle—the Imaginators.

GOLDEN QUEEN

Just when the Skylanders thought they'd seen the last of the Golden Queen, back she came as one of Master Eon's Sorcerer Class Senseis.

EMBER

Raised in the Dragonfire Dojo, Ember has spent most of her life training for battle. Highly gifted with her dual blades, she combines samurai skills with explosives to turn up the heat on evil.

KING PEN 👊

A muscle-bound penguin with some heavy-duty blade weapons, King Pen is the leader of the Senseis and a master of the Flipper-Fu fighting style.

AMBUSH 🗡️

A fearsome forest knight, Ambush is a master swordsman who uses his blades to protect the natural world from harm.

BUT WAIT, THERE'S MORE!

Even with the help of the Senseis, the Skylanders would have been no match for Kaos's Mind Magic and the Doomlanders. Luckily, Master Eon had one more trick up his sleeve . . .

INTRODUCING THE IMAGINATORS

Lord Kaos isn't the only one who can get creative, and it turns out that the Skylanders and Portal Masters are a pretty imaginative bunch, too.

Using Mind Magic and Imaginite, Portal Masters were able to create an entire new race of heroes dubbed the Imaginators, who the Senseis trained. Making them from a seemingly endless variety of features and equipping them with the most powerful weapons, armor, and abilities they could dream up, the Skylanders fought alongside the Imaginators to defeat the Doomlanders and ruin yet another of Kaos's evil plans.

SIR HOODINGTON

One of the most prominent Imaginators is the Fire Element knight
Sir Hoodington. With his spiked armor, Laserblade sword—and some
training from the Senseis—Sir Hoodington proved himself invaluable in
the fight against the Doomlanders. Portal Masters can use one of their
Imaginite Creation Crystals to conjure Sir Hoodington and all his armor.

Laserblade

Hooded Mystery

Double Guard

Shell Arms

Spike
Bracelets

Deep Sea Legs

Buckles and
Belts

Old Faithful Leg
Armor

WEAPONS

While many Skylanders rely on their unique special abilities to battle the forces of evil, some prefer to "tool up" with an assortment of weapons. Here are some of the more notable weapons in the Skylanders' arsenal.

TRIGGER HAPPY'S PISTOLS

Trigger Happy enjoys shooting so much that he custom-crafted a set of pistols, which—for reasons best known to himself—he specially adapted to shoot gold coins. When Trigger Happy is around, villains aren't concerned about hitting the jackpot so much as they're worried about the jackpot hitting *them*.

GILL GRUNT'S HARPOON GUN

When it comes to weaponry, Gill Grunt is armed to the . . . well, gills. Perhaps the most fearsome of all is his harpoon gun from which he can launch deadly harpoons at approaching enemies. Although, once they set eyes on the weapon, villains usually run *away* from Gill Grunt rather than towards him.

FRIGHT RIDER'S SPEAR

Whether being hurled at enemies, used like a jousting stick, or just swung about like a particularly pointy club, this long-handled spear is a giant thorn in evil's side. It has even been known to snag villains and drag them deep underground before zipping straight back to Rider's hand, ready to inflict more damage.

CHOP CHOP'S SWORD

What's worse than an Undead Arkeyan warrior wielding a sword? An Undead Arkeyan warrior wielding an *indestructible* sword. Sharp, pointy, and unbreakable, Chop Chop's ancient Arkeyan sword is one weapon you don't want to find yourself on the business end of.

DINO-RANG'S BOOMERANGS

In anyone else's hands, boomerangs might be pretty ineffective weapons against the mean and dangerous villains the Skylanders face. However, Dino-Rang's great skill means that these simple, curved pieces of stone become powerful enough to defeat any foe. As well as being used to attack enemies, the boomerangs can also form a protective shield—and even pick up food and treasure beyond Dino-Rang's reach.

HATS

In Skylands, hats are more than just a style choice. Sure, many of them help the Skylander-about-town look good, but they also serve a far more important function than that. If you ever spot a Skylander wearing a hat, you can be sure that they're gaining a useful power boost from it. Below is just a small selection of the headgear you might find balanced on a Skylander's bonce.

BIRTHDAY HAT

A traditional pointed paper hat with colorful spots and a frill on top, this jolly piece of headwear boosts the wearer's speed and critical hit ability.

FEZ

A fetching red number with a black tassel on top, donning the Fez gives the wearer an immediate Elemental Power increase.

DANGLING CARROT HAT

This unusual hat is made of a half coconut with a fork attached to it. The carrot on the fork helps motivate Skylanders to become faster and more powerful.

GLOOP HAT

Possibly the strangest hat of all, the Gloop Hat is a large, goo-like, one-eyed creature who seems perfectly content to sit on a Skylander's head for extended periods of time. Of course, it might just be a hat and not a living thing at all, but those pointy teeth sure are realistic . . .

VOLCANO HAT

You might assume that wearing a volcano on your head is an accident waiting to happen. Normally, you'd be right, but rather than burn the wearer alive with its molten lava, the Volcano Hat grants the wearer a number of useful benefits, including boosts to their speed and armor.

TREASURE & FOOD

If there's one thing the Skylanders love, it's protecting Skylands from the forces of evil. If there are two other things they love besides that, it's Treasure and Food. Although not necessarily in that order.

PERSEPHONE

Persephone is a Fairy Queen who uses her fairy magic to help Skylanders unlock their true potential.

In order to generate the vast quantities of magic required to upgrade the Skylanders, Persephone requires a constant supply of treasure. A basic upgrade will only cost a few shiny coins and maybe a diamond or two. If a Skylander really wants to power-up, though, they'd better have a big stash of cash they're willing to part with.

TREASURE

Scattered all across Skylands are treasures beyond your wildest dreams. Seriously, turn around in Skylands and you'll probably trip over a pile of gold, jewels, antique vases, and other priceless items. Where it all comes from and who it belongs to is anyone's guess, but the Skylanders are quick to put it to good use by trading it for strength boosts and skill upgrades that help them defeat whichever evil villain is getting up to no good at the time.

FOOD AND DRINK

Even after particularly grueling fights, Skylanders can regain their health by tearing into a delicious meal. By scoffing down a hot dog, slice of pizza, or—if they're feeling *really* brave—a fresh green vegetable, Skylanders can get themselves ready for battle almost immediately. And all that fighting helps burn calories, too, so they can eat what they like without worrying about unwanted weight gain.

SOUL GEMS

Hidden across Skylands are several magical gems, each one of which grants a unique ability to one specific Skylander. No one really knows where these gems came from or how they work. But as the abilities they grant the Skylanders are immensely powerful, the heroes always keep one eye open in case they should stumble upon a Soul Gem while out on a mission.

A BRIEF HISTORY OF SKYLANDS

Hello. I'm Hugo, the closest thing to an official historian we have here in Skylands. You see, much of Skylands' history is a mystery. I like to call it <u>hystery</u>, but as it sounds exactly the same, it's a joke that really only works when it is written down. Even then, as I've just discovered, it's not very funny.

Still I've been able to piece together an approximate timeline of major events simply by chatting with the Giants, asking Master Eon a few quick questions, and then reading several thousand books.

This may not be the ultimate definitive guide to Skylands' history (or <u>hystery</u>) but it's a good a place as any to start. I hope it proves useful.

Best wishes,

Hugo

P.S. Please don't let Flynn near it. He'll probably lose it, accidentally set it on fire, or both.

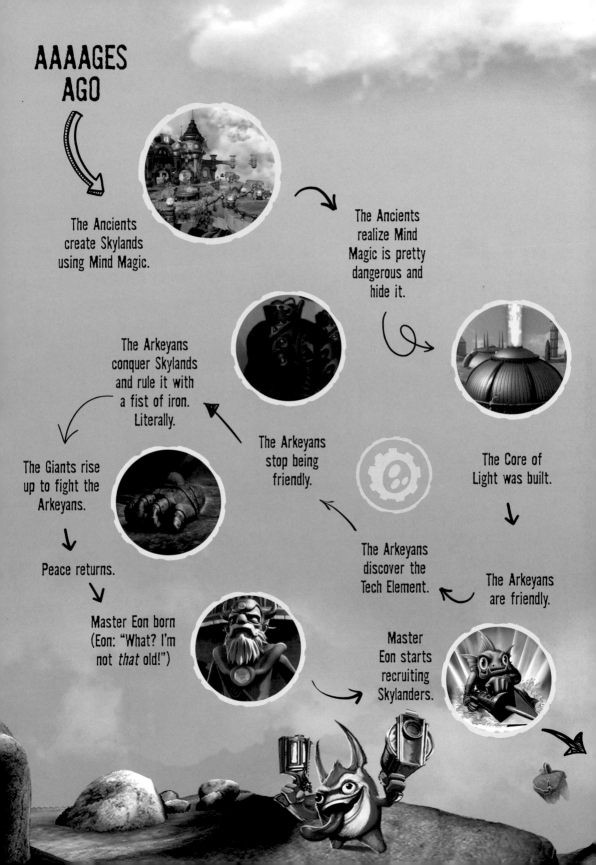

AAAAGES AGO

The Ancients create Skylands using Mind Magic.

The Ancients realize Mind Magic is pretty dangerous and hide it.

The Arkeyans conquer Skylands and rule it with a fist of iron. Literally.

The Giants rise up to fight the Arkeyans.

The Arkeyans stop being friendly.

The Core of Light was built.

Peace returns.

The Arkeyans discover the Tech Element.

The Arkeyans are friendly.

Master Eon born (Eon: "What? I'm not *that* old!")

Master Eon starts recruiting Skylanders.

MORE RECENT

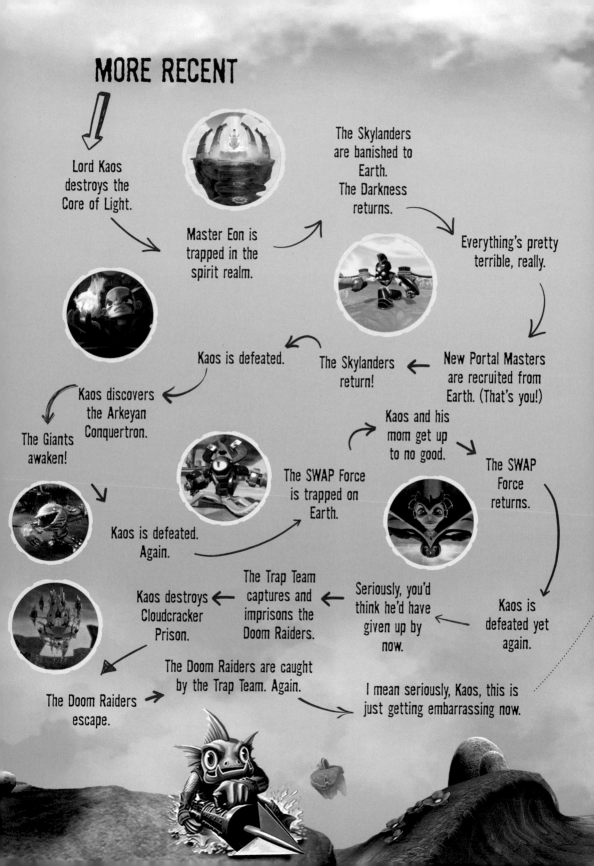

Lord Kaos destroys the Core of Light.

Master Eon is trapped in the spirit realm.

The Skylanders are banished to Earth. The Darkness returns.

Everything's pretty terrible, really.

New Portal Masters are recruited from Earth. (That's you!)

The Skylanders return!

Kaos is defeated.

Kaos discovers the Arkeyan Conquertron.

The Giants awaken!

Kaos and his mom get up to no good.

The SWAP Force returns.

The SWAP Force is trapped on Earth.

Kaos is defeated yet again.

Kaos is defeated. Again.

Seriously, you'd think he'd have given up by now.

The Trap Team captures and imprisons the Doom Raiders.

Kaos destroys Cloudcracker Prison.

The Doom Raiders are caught by the Trap Team. Again.

I mean seriously, Kaos, this is just getting embarrassing now.

The Doom Raiders escape.

NOW-ISH

The Doomstation of Ultimate Doomstruction is launched.

The SuperChargers drive, fly, and sail into action.

The Darkness forms an unholy alliance with Kaos.

Kaos uncovers Mind Magic.

Doomlanders are created.

Kaos is . . . I mean, do I even have to say it at this point?

Master Eon summons the Senseis to return.

Imaginators are created.

Kaos is defeated but probably not for the last time . . .

FAREWELL FROM MASTER EON

Well, there we have it, my young Portal Master—we have come to the end of our time together.

Have no fear, though. I have a feeling we shall meet again some time very soon. Kaos, the Darkness, and all manner of evil beings are still out there, skulking in the shadows, waiting for their next opportunity to strike. When they do, we'll need skilled, experienced Portal Masters like you to help keep Skylands safe.

Don't let the end of this book be the end of your quest for knowledge. Take what you have learned in these pages, pick up your portal, and plunge into adventure. Even in times of peace and calm, someone, somewhere always needs the help of a Skylander.

You're not going to let them down, are you?

Your friend,
Eon (Master)

INSIGHT KIDS

PO Box 3088
San Rafael, CA 94912
www.insighteditions.com

[f] Find us on Facebook: www.facebook.com/InsightEditions
[t] Follow us on Twitter: @insighteditions

ACTIVISION.

Library of Congress Cataloging-in-Publication Data available.

ISBN: 978-1-60887-954-0

Publisher: Raoul Goff
Associate Publisher: Jon Goodspeed
Art Director: Chrissy Kwasnik
Designer: Yousef Ghorbani
Associate Editor: Erum Khan
Managing Editor: Alan Kaplan
Production Editor: Lauren LePera
Associate Production Manager: Sam Taylor
Production Assistant: Sadie Crofts

Special thanks to Chris Bruno at Toys for Bob for all his help
contributing to this book.

ROOTS of PEACE   REPLANTED PAPER

Insight Editions, in association with Roots of Peace, will plant two
trees for each tree used in the manufacturing of this book. Roots
of Peace is an internationally renowned humanitarian organization
dedicated to eradicating land mines worldwide and converting war-torn
lands into productive farms and wildlife habitats. Roots of Peace will
plant two million fruit and nut trees in Afghanistan and provide farm-
ers there with the skills and support necessary for sustainable land use.

Manufactured in China by Insight Editions

10 9 8 7 6 5 4 3 2 1

ABOUT THE AUTHOR

Barry Hutchison is an award-winning author and comic-book
writer and a regular visitor to Skylands. Born and raised
in the remote Highlands of Scotland, Barry lives halfway
up a mountain with his wife, their two children, and a very
annoying dog. His biggest fear is that someday someone will
find out how much fun he is having writing books all day
and immediately put a stop to it. His second biggest fear is
squirrels.